Teddy's TV Troubles

Written by Joanne Cantor, Ph.D.

Illustrated by Tom Lowes

Goblin Fern Press, Inc.
Madison, Wisconsin

For information or to order additional copies please contact

www.joannecantor.com

or

Goblin Fern Press, Inc.

3809 Mineral Point Road, Madison, WI 53705

Toll-free: 888-670-BOOK (2665)   www.goblinfernpress.com

Quantity discounts available.

Library of Congress Cataloging-in-Publication Data

Cantor, Joanne.

Teddy's TV Troubles / written by Joanne Cantor ; illustrated by Tom Lowes. p. cm.

ISBN 0-9647663-7-X

1. Television and children. 2. Fear in children. I. Lowes, Tom, 1932-   II. Title.

HQ784.T4C265 2004

302.23'45'083--dc22

2004000930

Printed in the United States

10 9 8 7 6 5 4 3 2 1

Dedication

For Bob and Alex — *J C*

For Carole — *T L*

Acknowledgments

With gratitude to Kathleen DesMaisons for helping me to recognize the need for *Teddy's TV Troubles*, and to Melanie Friedersdorf Humphrey for her supportive mentoring about the process of creating children's books.

With special thanks to the students and staff of Heritage Elementary School in Waunakee, Wisconsin, especially the fourth graders, who enthusiastically contributed their outstanding art work to the first draft of *Teddy*. I am also grateful to the kindergartners at Heritage Elementary and the students at Woodland Montessori School, who gave useful feedback about the words and the images. They helped me make sure that the story made sense and that it hit the right tone.

Teddy Bear was scared.
Something he had seen on TV left him jittery and jumpy.

He didn't want to be alone.
He needed a hug!

Mommy Bear was puzzled.
"Tell me what it was that scared you," she said.

4

"I don't know," said Teddy.
"The way it looked. . . The way it sounded. . .
It was just scary."

5

Mommy took Teddy on her lap and said,
"I'm glad you told me, Teddy.
There are lots of scary things on TV.
The same thing happened to me
when I was your age."

"It *did?*" asked Teddy, looking surprised.
"What made *you* scared?"

6

"Well, I remember one time
there was something on the news,"
said Mommy. "Everyone was upset. . .

. . .and
another
time
I
saw
a
SCARY MOVIE."

"What did *you* do
when you were scared?" asked Teddy.

"Grandma and I sat down to talk about it," said Mommy.

9   "Sometimes, if what I saw was make-believe,
she told me why it could never happen to me.

Other times, if it was real, she showed me how
we could make sure it never happened to us. . .

But *always* she told me,
'Don't worry, honey.
No matter what happens, I will keep you safe.' "

"But Grandma knew that words don't always work,"
said Mommy.
"So we would draw pictures, too.
Would *you* like to draw pictures with *me?*"

"Yes, let's do it," said Teddy.

Teddy used his crayons
and drew a picture of what scared him.

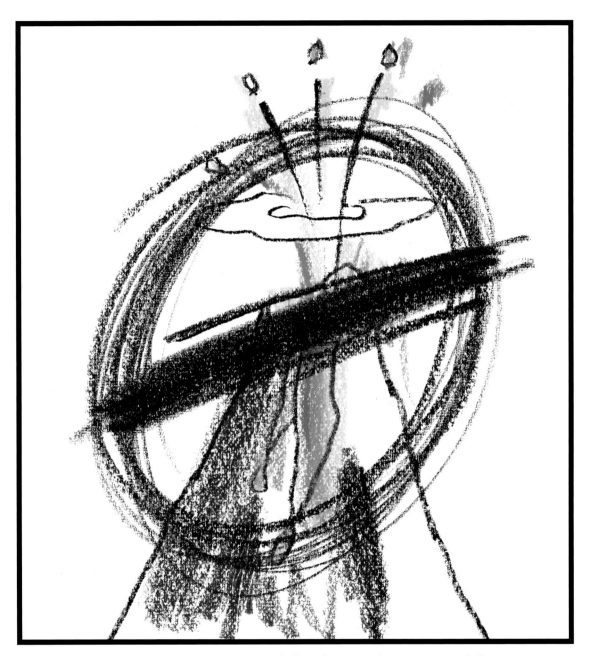

Then he decided to draw a black circle around his picture
and put a thick line through the middle of it.

Then Mommy drew a scary creature.

But she gave it a funny hat with flowers,
and drew a banana coming out of its ear.
Teddy laughed.

Then Teddy asked Mommy
to hide the pictures away inside a book.
They chose Teddy's thickest book
to keep the pictures safely inside.

Then they stacked ten more books
on top of that book. . .

After that, Teddy and Mommy took turns
drawing pictures of pretty things.
Teddy drew a beautiful scene of a sunshiny beach
with palm trees and sand castles.
They hung Teddy's picture on the fridge.

"I feel a little better already," said Teddy.
"But what did you do *next* when you were scared?"

"Sometimes we played with one of my favorite toys," said Mommy.
"Would you like to play with your building blocks?"

Teddy and Mommy built a big castle
with high walls.
Then they put Teddy's bunny,
Bunny, inside the castle to take a nap.

Teddy said to Bunny,
"Don't worry, Bunny.
No matter what happens
I will always keep you safe."

It was getting close to Teddy's bedtime.
"What if you still felt scared, Mommy,
and it was time to go to bed?" he asked.

23   "Sometimes I was worried that something scary
might be hiding in my room," said Mommy.

"Grandma always told me there was ***NO WAY***
it could be in my room.

Even so, if I still felt scared,
we looked around the room together anyway."

So Teddy and Mommy looked all around Teddy's room.
They looked under the desk
and under the bed
and even behind the clothes in the closet.

They looked everywhere
that anything could possibly hide.
But all they found was a dirty old sock
and a few little dust bunnies.

Nothing scary
at all.

26

27

"After Grandma and I looked around the room,"
said Mommy, "we would read a book about
a little bear who was scared.
Then Grandma would tuck me in bed with my favorite kitty, Kitty,
and she would hug and kiss Kitty and me goodnight."

So Mommy and Teddy read the book
about the little bear who was scared.
Then Teddy climbed into bed with Bunny.
"Grandma was pretty smart!" said Teddy with a smile.

And then Mommy kissed Teddy
and Bunny good night.

"Good night, Teddy!"

"Good night, Bunny!"

29

And Teddy and Bunny fell fast asleep.

About the Author

Joanne Cantor, Ph. D., is Professor Emerita of the University of Wisconsin-Madison,
where she spent 26 years teaching and doing research on the effects of the media on children.
She has published more than 80 scholarly articles and chapters, and she has worked with the National PTA,
the American Academy of Pediatrics, and the American Medical Association on projects related to children and television.
She has repeatedly testified before Congress and appears often in the national press and on
major television programs. She frequently lectures to parents, teachers, child-care providers,
and professional groups, and maintains an informational web site, www.joannecantor.com.
She lives in Madison, Wisconsin with her husband and teenage son.
The author welcomes your comments and questions (jrcantor@wisc.edu).

Other Books Written by Joanne Cantor:
"Mommy, I'm Scared": How TV and Movies Frighten Children and What We Can Do to Protect Them.
Harvest/Harcourt, 1998.

About the Illustrator

Tom Lowes has, among many artistic ventures, designed toys for Fisher-Price and illustrated packages and
Christmas stories for Lands' End of Dodgeville, Wisconsin. He lives near Madison, Wisconsin with wife, son, Airedale and paintbox.

Other Books Illustrated by Tom Lowes:
Casey's Four Holiday Celebrations by Kate Stormer
Goblin Fern Press, 2003.

Casey's Unexpected Friend by Kate Stormer
Goblin Fern Press, 2003.

Parents' Pointers
for Teddy's TV Troubles

When young children are frightened, words often don't work to comfort them. The best thing you can do is to provide your attention and warmth, and get your child involved in calming, soothing activities that you can enjoy together. This book provides a framework around which to help your child feel safe. You can simply read the book together or you can do some of the activities—like drawing pictures or building with blocks.

One thing that's so difficult about helping children with their fears is that some reasonable-sounding solutions can actually make the situation worse. Sometimes parents accidentally introduce a new fear that the child hasn't already thought about. This is why in *Teddy's TV Troubles*:

- There is no mention of what it was that was scary.
  Chances are that what scared your child is different anyway.

- There are no scary visual images.
  Visual images by themselves often frighten children greatly.

- Teddy's mother tells him that she was scared when she was a child
  so Teddy doesn't feel bad about admitting how he feels.

Children's fears can be hard to undo—a very frightened child will probably need your comforting attention repeatedly. The book and activities are meant to be used over and over again.

Teddy's TV Troubles is also intended to be enjoyed by children *before* they've been scared, so that they'll know what to do when they're frightened. It also works for children who have been frightened by something that didn't come from TV.

For more information on How TV and Movies Frighten Children and What We Can Do to Protect Them, see my parenting book "*Mommy, I'm Scared,*" and my web site, for parenting tips and other information, **www.joannecantor.com**.

Joanne Cantor, Ph.D.